QUAKING ASPEN

QUAKING ASPEN

A Carolrhoda Nature Watch Book

by Bonnie Holmes
photographs by Paula Jansen

Carolrhoda Books, Inc. / Minneapolis

To Joe, who lives life as an adventure, like a hike through an aspen forest —B.H.

To Ruth Berman, thank you for helping to guide me on the path of publishing and for making the process interesting and rewarding. I look forward to involvement with you on many exciting projects in the future. —P.J.

The author would like to give many thanks to the USDA Forest Service Southwestern Region, Rocky Mountain Forest and Range Experiment Station, Coconino National Forest, and Northern Arizona University School of Forestry, as well as Wildlife Biologist Greg Goodwin; Pathologist Mary Lou Fairweather; Botanist Barb Phillips, Ph.D.; Entomologist Jill Wilson, Ph.D.; Wildlife Biologist Heather Green; Silviculturist Rick Stahn; Archaeologist Peter Pilles; Assistant Professor of Forest Genetics Laura DeWald, Ph.D.; and Research Silviculturist Wayne Shepperd, Ph.D.

Carolrhoda Books, Inc., A Division of the Lerner Publishing Group
241 First Avenue North, Minneapolis, MN 55401 U.S.A.

Website address: www.lernerbooks.com

LIBRARY OF CONGRESS CATALOGING-IN-PUBLICATION DATA

Holmes, Bonnie.
    Quaking aspen / by Bonnie Holmes; photographs by Paula Jansen.
      p.   cm.
    "A Carolrhoda nature watch book."
    Includes index.
    Summary: Describes the life-cycle of the quaking aspen, its role in the ecosystem, and the threat to aspens from animals and people.
    ISBN 1–57505–351–9 (alk. paper)
    1. Populus tremuloides—West (U.S.)—Juvenile literature.
    2. Populus tremuloides—Ecology—West (U.S.)—Juvenile literature.
    3. Forest ecology—West (U.S.)—Juvenile literature. [1. Aspen.
    2. Trees. 3. Forest ecology. 4. Ecology.] I. Jansen, Paula, ill. II. Title.
    QK495.S16H66 1999
    583'.65 — dc21   98-31909

Manufactured in the United States of America
1 2 3 4 5 6 – JR – 04 03 02 01 00 99

CONTENTS

INTRODUCTION

It's autumn in the mountains of the West. Colorful leaves carpet the forest floor and crunch as squirrels skitter over them in their hurry to gather food for the winter. Squishy mushrooms of many sizes and shapes have popped up from the moist ground. Each passing day is shorter than the last.

Above: *Early in the autumn, a quaking aspen grove in Arizona begins to glow with color.*
Right: *By winter, the trunks and branches of the same grove stand out against the dark pines behind them.*

Graceful aspen trees sway with the gentle breezes. Their light-colored trunks stand out against the dark wood of the pines. For a few weeks, their round, fluttering leaves offer a spectacular display of gold, orange, and red—the shades of the sunset.

The wind gets stronger. The air feels colder. Winter is near—a time of rest in the forest. More leaves float to the ground. The forest gets darker. We leave the woods and head inside, knowing that this magical season will return to us year after year.

But our great quaking aspen groves, which have been recreating themselves for centuries, may not return to us year after year. They are in danger of disappearing.

MOTHERS OF THE FOREST

Aspen trees need the sun to grow. Unlike spruces, firs, and maples, quaking aspens don't grow as well in the shade. But in open, sunlit meadows, aspens usually grow 6 to 12 inches (15–30 cm) each year. As they grow, they change the environment beneath their swaying branches. The shade they provide cools the air and soil below them, allowing grasses, wildflowers, and fir trees to grow and thrive. Because they nurture the land and create an environment for other plants and animals to live in, aspen trees are often referred to as "the mothers of the forest."

Quaking aspen is also known as trembling aspen, American aspen, smalltooth aspen, or simply aspen. It is called quaking or trembling because of the way its paper-thin leaves shake in the slightest breeze. Its **petioles**, the leaf stems, are slender and flat. The broad, round leaves are thin and flat. Both the leaves and the petioles catch the wind and flutter. Fluttering in the wind helps the leaves escape the full heat of the sun. It keeps them from drying out.

Scientists have given the quaking aspen, and all plants and animals, a specific scientific name so that people all over the world will be able to recognize them. For the quaking aspen, that name is *Populus tremuloides.* "Tremuloides" sounds a bit like trembles, which is a good description of how the leaves move.

Right: *An aspen's flat leaves and petioles catch the wind and cause the leaves to flutter.*

Another kind of aspen is the bigtooth aspen—*Populus grandidentata*. It looks a lot like the quaking aspen, except its leaves are larger. In many places, quaking aspens and bigtooth aspens grow next to each other, but the quaking aspen trees are found in many more places and can make up an entire, huge forest by themselves.

Cottonwoods, which have seeds that float on the air like wisps of cotton, and poplars are the closest relatives of aspens. They all have light-colored bark. Aspens, cottonwoods, and poplars are all members of the willow family.

The tall, thin poplar is a close relative of the quaking aspen.

The Quaking Aspen in North America

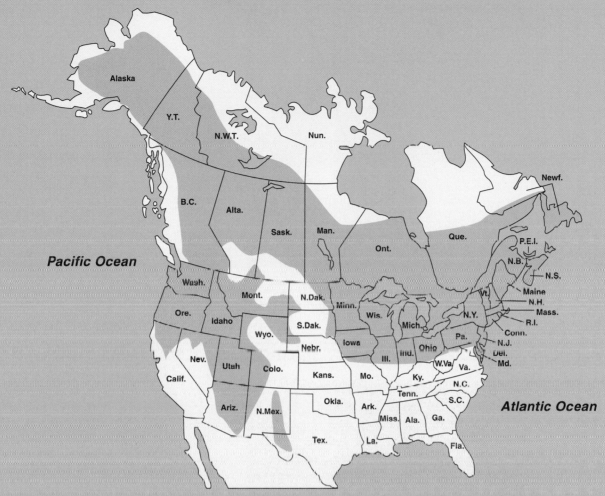

The quaking aspen grows in the Northern Hemisphere. In North America, the tree is found in the gold areas.

If you looked down on Earth from high above the North Pole, you would find aspen trees all around the Northern Hemisphere. In North America, the quaking aspen grows in more places than any other tree. It is found throughout Canada, up to the edge of the frigid Alaskan tundra, across the northeastern United States, and along the western mountain ranges to Mexico.

In many parts of the United States, aspens often grow in forests with many other types of trees. Their white bark lights up the woods in scattered stands, or groups of trees. But New Mexico, Arizona, Wyoming, Colorado, and Utah have large forests made up primarily of quaking aspens.

THE GROWING ASPEN

Like most plants, aspens are able to make their own food. They use a green compound in their leaves called **chlorophyll.** With chlorophyll, they take energy from the sun and combine it with carbon dioxide from the air and water from the ground to create **glucose,** or sugary plant food, and oxygen. The trees don't need the oxygen, so they release it into the air. The entire food-producing process is called **photosynthesis.**

Aspen trees are very sensitive to changes in sunlight and a drop in temperature. When the days get shorter, the leaves stop making chlorophyll. This slows down the food-producing processes and prepares the tree for winter.

Aspens are **deciduous** trees. This means they shed their leaves, but not before dressing up the countryside with a striking display of golds, oranges, and reds. From about mid-September to mid-October, aspen leaves turn from bright green to the sunset hues of autumn.

Chlorophyll makes aspen leaves bright green (upper left). Without chlorophyll, aspen leaves can be shades of yellow, gold, and orange (left).

During the cold months, it is difficult to tell whether an aspen is dead or alive. The bare trunks might remind you of soldiers in white uniforms standing at attention. But even without leaves, aspens add luster to the dark of winter with their light-colored bark.

Like most plants, aspens rely on their leaves to produce chlorophyll, but their bark helps out, too. It also contains chlorophyll. Beneath the whitish outside bark, the inner bark layer is green. This inner layer allows the aspen tree to manufacture food for itself all year—even during the winter when it has no leaves. This helps the aspen grow faster, especially in extremely cold climates and high up in the mountains where the growing season for most plants is very short.

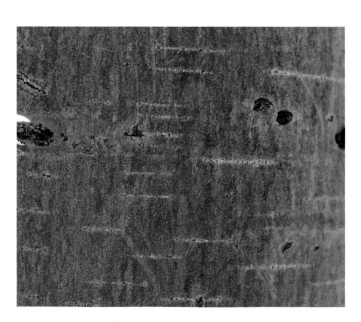

Even in winter, the chlorophyll in aspen trunks helps the trees to grow.

The outer layer of bark protects the layers of wood inside.

Trees show their age in the rings of a trunk's cross section. Each ring represents one year. The weather in each year is shown by the size of each ring. For example, during a drought, the tree rings are narrower and appear closer together than during a wet period when the tree was well nourished.

Bark is the outer protective covering of a tree. In aspen trees, the bark is very thin and soft. It is made up of cells that have died and have been pushed to the outside of the tree. Unlike the bark of other trees, such as pines and oaks, the bark of the aspen is not thick or strong enough to protect the tree from fire.

Inside the outer layer of bark is a layer of living cells called the **phloem** (FLOW-um). The tree's glucose is carried from the leaves down to the roots by the phloem. The next layer is the **cambium.** Cambium cells produce new cells and make the tree grow bigger and stronger each year.

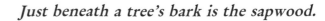

Just beneath a tree's bark is the sapwood.

The new cells either become phloem cells or **xylem** (ZY-lum) cells, which make up the wood itself. Xylem cells carry **sap**—water and nutrients—from the roots of the tree upward and outward to the branches and treetop.

The outer part of the xylem is called the **sapwood**. The inner part of the xylem is called the **heartwood**. The

heartwood is stronger and darker than the sapwood. It is considered the backbone of the tree. Heartwood is darker partly because of its **resin,** an oily protective substance. Resin hardens when it is exposed to air, forming a scablike covering over wounds in the tree.

Trees are considered hardwoods or softwoods depending on the structure of the cells in the tree trunk. **Conifers,** or cone-bearing trees, such as pines and firs, are softwoods. Flowering trees, such as aspen and oak, are hardwoods. Oddly enough, the wood of aspen trees is actually much softer than the wood of some so-called softwood trees.

MAKING NEW ASPENS

Each spring, aspen trees bear flowers. These flowers come in clusters that look like pink caterpillars. These are called **catkins.** Later in the spring and early summer, the aspen's new flat, thin leaves sprout very quickly, covering the tree branches with rich bouquets of green.

Aspen trees are either male or female. Female trees have pistil-bearing flowers. The pistil is where seeds are made. Male trees have stamen-bearing flowers. The stamens shake pollen out into the air.

Clusters of aspen flowers are fluffy, pinkish catkins (left). *Aspen buds begin to sprout* (above).

17

Wind carries the pollen to the pistil-bearing catkins, where the pollen fertilizes the seeds. Aspen pollen looks like dry, yellow dust.

When pollen fertilizes the catkins with pistils, the catkins develop into little capsules. Soon they release small seeds, which have little white hairs. The hairs help the seeds sail on the breeze to a new location.

Fluffy and white, the seeds look like cotton balls piling up on the forest floor. It takes a lot of energy for an aspen tree to produce catkins and seeds, but very few of the seeds will develop into seedlings. In order for an aspen tree to grow from a seed, the seed has to land on bare, moist soil. There are not many places in the forest where the ground is open, moist, and receiving enough sunlight.

So aspen trees usually reproduce in a different way. They clone themselves. They are able to produce exact replicas of themselves without the union of a male parent and a female parent. These replicas have the same genes, the basic chemical units in the cells of every living thing that determine its various characteristics.

Fluffy, white aspen seeds land on bare soil (upper left) *and the surface of a pond* (left).

All of us are created from our parents. People might say that you have your mother's almond-shaped eyes or your father's dark hair. You have a combination of genes from your mother and your father. Clones have only one parent. They have received all of their genes from that parent. So a clone and its parent are identical twins, except they are different ages.

Scientists have figured out how to clone plants and animals, but aspen trees have always been cloning themselves. When aspens clone themselves, new shoots, or **suckers,** spring up from buds on the aspen's shallow root system, which curls and tangles beneath the surface of the ground.

Sometimes the buds on these roots lie **dormant,** or inactive, for years. When there is plenty of open ground and sunlight available, a new aspen will start to grow. This is why aspen trees sometimes appear unexpectedly. If aspen trees are growing in one backyard, their roots may find their way under fences and into a neighboring yard, surprising the neighbors with the young shoots and buds of a new aspen tree. These young aspens are fed and watered by the fully formed root system of their parent tree. This helps them survive in great weather extremes.

An aspen clone sprouts from a root growing under a wooden deck.

You can identify aspen clones by looking very closely at the trees. All of the branches will be growing at the same angle from the trunks. Clones can be easily spotted in the autumn when aspen leaves change colors, because at the same time, the leaves of one tree will change to the same color as the leaves of its clones. So an aspen grove may have big patches of bright gold from one group of clones, and red, burnt orange, and yellow green from other groups.

A grove of aspen clones lights up the forest in autumn.

An ancient clone has spread over a mountain valley.

Since aspen trees have been cloning themselves for thousands of years, a living aspen tree may have an identical twin that lived thousands of years earlier. Researchers have compared aspen leaves with ancient aspen leaves that have been preserved as fossils. They say it is possible that some aspens in the western United States may be clones of aspens that lived millions of years ago!

One very old, enormous clone is growing in the Wasatch Mountains of Utah. It has been named Pando, a Latin word that means "I spread." Indeed, Pando has spread. It has 47,000 tree trunks—all of them genetically identical—covering 106 acres (43 hectares). Some scientists believe Pando is the world's largest living organism.

IN AN ASPEN GROVE

Aspen trees usually grow up to a foot taller each year, but they can shoot up as much as 5 feet (1.5 m) taller in a particularly good growing season. As they grow, the newer upper branches block the sunlight from the lower branches. The lower branches eventually die and break off. When they do, they leave behind dark scars on the trunks that look like giant eyes.

Leaves on upper branches block the sunlight in a densely growing aspen grove (left). *The remains of a branch look like an eye on the aspen trunk* (above).

Aspens rarely grow to be taller than 70 feet (21 m) or older than 200 years. By the time they get to be about 100 years old, they may be taller than a three-story building and 1 to 2 feet thick (30–60 cm). When aspen trees get to be this big and old, the stand becomes particularly vulnerable to heavy winds. The aspens' roots are often weakened by disease and are no longer strong enough to anchor the heavy trees. Every so often, a windstorm will send a group of the huge white trunks crashing to the ground.

A heavy wind could blow down the trees in this old aspen grove.

Forces are always at work weakening the trees. A fungus called **false tinder** grows on aspens. It attacks the tree from the inside of the trunk and eats away at the wood. If an aspen has this fungus, a round gray patch called a **conk** will appear on the outside of the tree in old branch scars. The conk is the fruiting part of the fungus. Conks look like elephant knees and may appear in many places on one tree. Through the conks, spores are released into the air—spores that may land on openings in other aspens and grow into fungi on the trunks of those trees.

An aspen can survive for a long time with false tinder. In the meantime, the false tinder is hollowing out the trunk, creating cavities—or holes—in the tree. The cavities may become homes for families of small birds.

When aspens die, they don't always fall to the ground right away. **Snags,** or standing dead trees, provide protection for squirrels, chipmunks, bats, and small birds. The great raptors, birds of prey such as hawks and owls, use the upper branches of snags as a place to perch. Without leaves in their way, the large birds can use their incredibly powerful eyesight to spot their prey from this seat high above the forest floor.

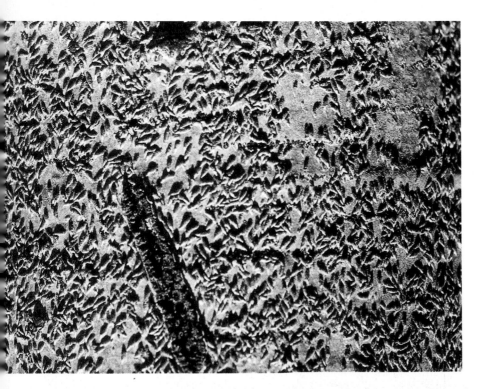

Left: *Oyster shell scale, an insect, damages the trunk of an aspen tree.*
Right: *From the top of this snag, a large bird could survey the rest of the forest.*

Whether dead or alive, aspens are used by hundreds of different kinds of wildlife. Hungry **herbivores**—animals such as deer, elk, and snowshoe hares that feed on grasses and shrubs—eat young aspen sprouts. Different clones have different flavors, so browsing animals prefer certain aspen groves over others. Through the cold winter months, the aspen's green, nutritious inner bark sustains many creatures of the forest when food is scarce. You can tell when elk have been munching on an aspen tree by the rows of bite marks on the trunks.

Deer browse at the edge of an aspen grove (left) *and leave rows of bite marks on the trunks* (above).

The open land around a beaver pond is an ideal place for quaking aspens to grow.

With little effort, animals can break into the soft bark of the aspen tree with their teeth. Beavers will chomp through the white trunks and drag the logs to streams where they use them to dam up the water. Later, they will gnaw on the wood for food.

Beavers and aspens benefit each other. Eventually, the ponds created by the large rodents dry up. When that happens, a marshy meadow is created. The open, fertile land is a great place for quaking aspens to grow.

After a sapsucker does its work, sap oozes from the tree.

Woodpeckers make holes in aspen trunks. When a woodpecker drills into a tree, the tree's sweet sap oozes out. Insects are attracted to the sap, but once they touch the sticky substance, they are stuck. The birds that come along can snatch them up for a quick meal.

A woodpecker known as a sapsucker makes small holes that trap insects. People used to think the bird drank the sap.

That's how the bird got its name. But the sapsucker was really eating the trapped insects.

Woodpeckers seem to know when an aspen is sick or dying. They prefer to work on those trees because the wood of a decaying tree is softer and easier to hollow out. With a noisy rat-a-tat tapping against the tree, a woodpecker pecks through the bark and into the tree to create a space big enough to fit a whole woodpecker family.

The woodpecker is called a primary nester because it makes a hole in the tree and is the first creature to use it. The woodpecker lays its eggs and nurtures its babies in the hole it has made. When the baby woodpeckers have learned to fly and have left the nest, the woodpecker family leaves its home.

The cavity does not go to waste, however, because another bird will move in the next spring to lay its eggs and raise its young. Birds such as swallows, nuthatches, and bluebirds are considered secondary nesters because they use the holes after the work has been done by the woodpecker. Meanwhile, the woodpecker will peck a hole in a different tree when it is ready to lay more eggs.

When an aspen tree dies and falls to the ground, squirrels, mice, and gophers start to use it. The hollow places in the trunk made by fungi and woodpeckers provide perfect hiding spots for the small animals and good storage areas for food.

Once a tree is on the ground, tiny microorganisms help break it down, gradually releasing the tree's nutrients back into the soil. Insects such as termites and carpenter ants burrow through the wood. They make tunnels that allow air and water to pass through. In these moist, dark passages, more fungi and molds begin to grow. Snails and slugs are attracted to the moisture and eat the fungi. Centipedes and millipedes hide in the trunk. There they can catch small insects. Lichens and moss begin to grow on the bark.

A small snake wriggles along a rotting log.

In a few years, all of this activity turns the tree into a soft, spongy log. Animals running over it and through it further break the wood into tiny bits. Worms, constantly churning through the decayed wood, work the tree bits back into the soil until all the nutrients that helped the tree grow have returned to the earth. Soil containing decayed plant and animal matter is called **humus.** The rich humus in aspen forests helps many different kinds of plants, from tiny wildflowers to towering quaking aspens, grow.

Nutrients from decomposing logs go back into the soil and help aspen trees grow. Small animals use the rotting logs for shelter and as a place to store food. That's why wildlife biologists say there's life in dead trees.

WILDFIRE

The **ecosystem**—the natural system of plants and animals that function as a unit—of the dry western forests includes fire. Following the drying days of early summer, monsoon rains play upon the thirsty land, bringing with them lightning shows so intense that dramatic flashes illuminate a moonless night. Often, when lightning strikes a tree, fire pours onto the forest floor.

Fed by grasses and shrubs, the fire spreads through the woods. It acts as nature's housekeeper—cleaning up dead debris such as pine needles and branches. It burns sick and dying plants—releasing and recycling the nutrients that were once stored in their bark and stems.

Young aspens grow quickly in the fertile soil left from a forest fire.

When the fire burns itself out or is extinguished by rain, large openings remain in the forest. Sunlight can then reach all the way to the ground and provide the perfect setting for aspen trees to flourish.

Because aspen trees are among the first plants to grow after a fire or windstorm has swept over the land, the aspen is an **early succession** species, or pioneering plant. Their job in the ecosystem is to shoot up in an open area, grow very fast, provide shade, and prepare the soil for a great variety of plants.

As young aspen trees begin to regenerate the forest, there is still plenty of sunlight, but the small trees provide some shade. Ferns and wildflowers begin to grow around the base of the aspens. Yellow columbines, pink and white wild geraniums, and bright red wild strawberries are some of the plants that grow in aspen forests.

As the plant life becomes thicker, it becomes important to animals such as wild turkeys, who hide from danger in the grasses and build nests on the ground. Plant life is also important to larger animals such as deer. They, too, hide in the lush vegetation and feel safe there when they give birth to their fawns.

A fawn hides (above) *and ferns flourish* (left) *in the cool shade beneath aspen trees.*

Conifer seedlings also grow in the cool shade provided by the quick-growing aspen trees. In time, the pines and firs grow taller than the aspens and begin to shut out the sunlight. Without intense sunlight, the aspen trees die and the conifers take over, creating a thick, dark forest of evergreens.

As the tall conifers get bigger and stronger, the aspens slowly begin to disappear from the forest . . . until fire comes through again, creating openings that allow sunlight to reach the forest floor, which signals aspen roots to sprout.

Conifers tower over a stand of aspens.

ASPENS AND PEOPLE

Like all trees, aspens are natural air filters. They rid the atmosphere of the carbon dioxide that comes from all animals, including humans, when they exhale. Carbon dioxide is also put into the air by exhaust from cars and factories. Trees use carbon dioxide, and they replenish the air with oxygen, which is what all animals need to survive. Trees are essential for our survival.

People have used aspen trees for centuries. The American Indians who inhabited northern Arizona from around A.D. 650 to 1400 survived despite the dry mountain climate. They are called Sinagua after the Spanish words *sin agua*—meaning "without water." The Sinagua used aspen logs in their buildings. The straight, long aspen trunks were ideal for roof beams and posts.

Aspen logs were once used as support beams in ancient dwellings such as these.

American Indians and pioneers chewed on the bark of aspens, willows, and cottonwoods to make the pain of a toothache go away. The bark of these trees contains a substance that is similar to aspirin.

Early pioneers and Spanish, Mexican, and Basque sheepherders carved messages into the bark of aspen trees. Some of these messages have been preserved as historic markers.

A message carved in an aspen tree in 1915 is preserved as a historic marker.

More recent messages carved into the bark of trees are considered graffiti, however. The marks not only mess up the woods, but they are harmful to the tree trunks. A cut on a tree is much like a cut on our skin. Through the open wound, the tree can become infected. Openings in the bark also allow insects to enter and damage the tree.

Harmful **canker fungi** are able to attack the tree this way. They invade the cambium and girdle, or encircle, the aspen trunk. Eventually they can choke off the flow of water to the tree and kill it.

As firewood, aspen cuts easily and catches on fire quickly. The wood burns fast and gives off very little creosote, an oily tarlike substance that forms from resin. Creosote buildup can be a big problem, as it sometimes clogs chimneys and woodstove pipes and can contribute to chimney fires.

The aspen's heartwood, the strongest and most valuable part of the tree, is used to make furniture, frames, beams, and boards. Aspen wood is also used to make boxes, crates, matches, and paper.

More recent carvings are thought of as graffiti.

Perhaps most of all, people love quaking aspens for their sheer beauty, the variety of wildlife they attract, and the many different plants that grow around them. The shade provided by full-grown quaking aspens, along with the soft rustling of their leaves, makes the perfect setting for warm-weather picnics, wildlife viewing, scenic hikes, and mountain biking. But on very windy days, aspen groves should be avoided because the trees are so easily blown down. In popular, well-used areas, snags are often cut so that they don't come crashing to the ground and hurt somebody or block a road or trail.

At one time, snags were not valued for their benefit to wildlife. Foresters worked to cut them all down. It was also thought that snags attracted lightning, which could lead to forest fires. Foresters have since learned that standing dead trees act no more as lightning rods than living trees. But when they are struck by lightning, their dead wood burns more easily than the wood of living trees.

Left: *A child enjoys her family's hike through an aspen grove.*
Right: *A snag towers over a young aspen clone flourishing in a sunlit clearing.*

PLIGHT OF THE QUAKING ASPEN

As much as quaking aspens are an essential part of our ecosystem, there is concern that great groves of these trees are becoming endangered. Over a 24-year period, an inventory of aspen groves revealed an astounding drop in the number of these graceful trees. In 1962, there were 486,000 acres (197,000 hectares) of aspens in Arizona and New Mexico. By 1986, the number was slashed nearly in half, to 263,000 acres (106,000 hectares).

Since then, researchers have taken a closer look at aspen forests and found similar changes. On Monroe Mountain in Utah, most of a 14,000-acre (5,700-hectare) area had been an aspen forest 150 years ago. By 2000, more than half of the aspens had disappeared. When the researchers looked at the entire state of Utah, they found that 60 percent of Utah's aspen forests had been taken over by pines, firs, and sagebrush. What's more, they concluded that most of the aspen ecosystems that still exist will eventually disappear.

With more people living in the West, quaking aspen stands are shrinking and numbers of the trees are dropping.

What happened to the quaking aspens? The aspens are disappearing for many reasons. In areas where elk, deer, sheep, and cattle compete for food, young aspen groves have trouble getting established. As soon as the delicate limbs sprout a bud, these browsing animals often come along to chomp the tender new growth right off. Young aspen saplings need 10 to 15 years of protection before they grow above the reach of an elk—about 15 feet high (45 m). To give the aspen groves a fighting chance to grow and survive, foresters sometimes build "exclosure" fences to keep the animals out.

Elk and deer affect aspens in other ways, too. Each summer, their new antlers are covered by a soft skin called velvet. As the antlers grow, the velvet starts to shed. To rub the velvet off, elk and deer scrape their antlers against aspen and other kinds of trees. This can make the bark fall off and leave large, bare, unprotected spots where insects and diseases can easily attack the trees.

Deer and elk feed on tasty aspen sprouts (above) *and wear away aspen bark* (right) *by rubbing their antlers against it.*

Without even knowing it, people have had a negative impact on aspen trees. For more than a hundred years, we've been putting out forest fires as fast as we can to protect lives and property. When we think about forest fires, we usually think they are harmful to the forest, but we have learned that fire actually helps quaking aspens. Researchers believe Pando got to be so big and so old because of the many fires over its lifetime. When stems die from fire or other causes, aspen roots send up new shoots.

A firefighter's helicopter carries water to a fire.

As the open lands of the West have become settled, fire no longer is allowed to play its natural role in the ecosystem. Conifer forests have entirely taken over many quaking aspen forests.

It is a normal part of forest succession for conifers to replace aspens. The prob-lem is that there are fewer and fewer sun-lit openings for aspens to grow back. With fewer aspen trees, there are fewer active suckers. Eventually, the suckers die. Once a clone is gone, that unique genetic material is lost forever.

Fire, or another kind of major disturbance like a windstorm, is necessary for the aspen trees to sprout. If nature cannot provide this disturbance and create bright, sun-drenched openings in the thick woods, the effects of nature need to be mimicked to ensure a healthy forest and the continued existence of aspens.

One of the ways foresters mimic nature is by cutting trees or allowing logging companies to buy and harvest the timber. Sometimes families are invited into an area in November and December to cut their own Christmas trees. These types of tree-cutting programs keep the aspen groves from being taken over by conifers.

Prescribed burns are used to bring fire back into the ecosystem in a controlled way. Just as a doctor prescribes medicine for a sick person, foresters prescribe treatments for an unhealthy forest. Prescribed burns are fires that are lit on purpose and watched carefully. Foresters check the weather and the amount of moisture there is in the woods before setting the fires to make sure they don't spread out of control.

A firefighter puts out the fire at the edge of a prescribed burn.

A tall, full-grown aspen grove or aspen forest only survives for about one hundred years if young aspen trees do not replace the older ones. That's a very short life span for trees in a forest, as pines live two hundred to three hundred years and oaks can live twice that long.

To make sure aspen trees continue to flourish, it is important that we understand how they grow and what they need. The more we know about how the many parts of our ecosystems work and how they work together, the better for the future of these natural treasures.

GLOSSARY

cambium: a thin layer of cells beneath the phloem that produces new living cells and helps a tree grow

canker fungi: a fungus that encircles a tree trunk

catkins: clusters of flowers that bud on trees in spring

chlorophyll: the green chemical in plants that combines with light to change water and carbon dioxide into plant food

conifers: trees that produce needles and cones

conk: the fruiting body of a fungus

deciduous: a type of tree that loses its leaves every autumn and grows new ones each spring

dormant: temporarily inactive

early succession: the first plants to grow back after a fire or windstorm

ecosystems: communities of animals and plants that function as a unit in nature

false tinder: a fungus found in aspens that eats away at the wood

glucose: sugar that is produced and used as food by green plants

heartwood: a tree's inner core—the backbone of the tree

herbivores: plant-eating animals

humus: rich dark soil made from decayed plant and animal matter

petiole: a leaf's stem, which sprouts from a branch and runs through the middle of a leaf to its tip

phloem: a thin layer of living cells beneath the bark that carries glucose from leaves to roots

photosynthesis: a plant's way of using sunlight to make food and oxygen out of water and carbon dioxide

prescribed burns: controlled fires that are lit on purpose to burn away sick and dead plant matter

resin: an oily protective substance produced by trees and plants

sap: liquid that flows through a plant, carrying water and nutrients

sapwood: the living cells on the outer part of the xylem that carry sap

snags: dead trees that stand in forests

suckers: new shoots that spring up on tree roots and eventually become new trees

xylem: the woody inner core of a tree that carries water and nutrients from roots to leaves

INDEX

ABOUT THE AUTHOR

Bonnie Holmes has spent some 15 years in the news business working as a television news producer, news director, anchor, and reporter. She has written several documentaries, including "Exploring Lake Powell," which appears on PBS, and "Our Great Ponderosa Pine Forest—Restoring the Balance," used in college and university classes. Bonnie has received nine Associated Press awards for news writing and reporting. Her love for the outdoors, and especially the magic of aspen forests, inspired her to write *Quaking Aspen* to share with children everywhere. Bonnie runs her own public relations firm and looks forward to writing more books. She lives in the mountain town of Flagstaff, Arizona, with her husband, Joe, sons Tyler and Logan, and a giant yellow lab named Lacy.

ABOUT THE PHOTOGRAPHER

Paula Jansen lives in northern Arizona with her husband and two children. She is an active member of ASMP—American Society of Media Photographers, Inc. She also enjoys working in large-format photography.

Healthy Eating

Meat and Protein

Nancy Dickmann

Heinemann Library
Chicago, Illinois

www.heinemannraintree.com
Visit our website to find out
more information about
Heinemann-Raintree books.

To order:

☎ Phone 888-454-2279

💻 Visit www.heinemannraintree.com
to browse our catalog and order online.

Edited by Siân Smith, Nancy Dickmann, and Rebecca Rissman
Designed by Joanna Hinton-Malivoire
Picture research by Elizabeth Alexander
Production by Victoria Fitzgerald
Originated by Capstone Global Library Ltd
Printed and bound in China by South China Printing Company Ltd

ISBN 978-1-4329-3981-6
14 13 12 11 10
10 9 8 7 6 5 4 3 2 1

Library of Congress Cataloging-in-Publication Data

Dickmann, Nancy.
  Meat and protein / Nancy Dickmann.
     p. cm. -- (Healthy eating)
  Includes bibliographical references and index.
  ISBN 978-1-4329-3981-6 (hc) -- ISBN 978-1-4329-3988-5 (pb) 1. Meat--
Juvenile literature. 2. Proteins in human nutrition--Juvenile literature. I. Title.
  QP144.M43D53 2011
  613.2'82--dc22
                              2009045482

Acknowledgements
We would like to thank the following for permission to reproduce
photographs: © Capstone Publishers pp.**5**, **12**, **14**, **22** (Karon Dubke);
Corbis p.**13** (© Image Source); Getty Images pp.**4** (Kevin Summers/
Photographer's Choice), **10** (Inga Spence/Visuals Unlimited), **11** (Dorling
Kindersley), **21** (Jon Feingersh/Iconica); iStockphoto pp.**8** (© Ronald
Fernandez), **23 top** (© Mark Hatfield); Photolibrary pp.**7** (Jo Whitworth/
Garden Picture Library), **9** (Animals Animals/Robert Maier), **20** (Peter
Mason/Cultura); Shutterstock pp.**6** (© BESTWEB), **15**, **23 middle** (© Juriah
Mosin), **16** (© a9photo), **17**, **23 bottom** (© Joe Gough), **18** (© Monkey
Business Images); USDA Center for Nutrition Policy and Promotion p.**19**.

Front cover photograph of meat, fish, eggs, nuts, and beans reproduced
with permission of © Capstone Publishers (Karon Dubke). Back cover
photograph reproduced with permission of iStockphoto (© Ronald
Fernandez).

We would like to thank Dr Sarah Schenker for her invaluable help in the
preparation of this book.

Every effort has been made to contact copyright holders of material
reproduced in this book. Any omissions will be rectified in subsequent
printings if notice is given to the publishers.

Contents

Meat and beans are foods that
we eat.

We also eat fish, eggs, and nuts.

Meat comes from animals such as cows.

Beans come from plants.

tuna

Fish comes from animals such as tuna.

Eggs come from birds such
as chickens.

Nuts grow on trees.

Eating these foods can keep
us healthy.

Helping Your Body

Meat, fish, eggs, beans, and nuts all have protein.

You need protein to grow.

Eating beans gives you energy.

You need energy to work and play.

fish

Eating meat and fish helps keep your blood healthy.

Some meat has a lot of fat. Too much fat can hurt your body.

Healthy Eating

We need to eat different kinds of food each day.

The food pyramid tells us to eat foods from each food group.

19

We eat meat and other protein foods to stay healthy.

We eat these foods because they taste good!

Find the Meat

Here is a healthy dinner. Can you find a food made from meat?

Answer on page 24

Picture Glossary

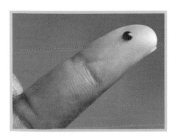 **blood** red liquid inside your body. Blood takes food and air to all your body parts.

 **energy** the power to do something. We need energy when we work or play.

 **fat** oily thing in some foods. Your body uses fat to keep warm. Eating too much fat is bad for your body.

Index

Answer to quiz on page 22: The meat food is chicken.

Notes for parents and teachers

Before reading

Explain that we need to eat a range of different foods to stay healthy. Introduce the meat and beans food group. Our bodies use protein from meat and beans to help build many of our body parts including our skin, hair, muscles, bones, and blood. Protein helps our bodies grow.

After reading

- Discuss the fact that some people do not eat meat and fish (vegetarians) and some do not eat meat, fish, eggs, or dairy (vegans). Brainstorm other foods they can eat to make sure they get enough protein.
- Explain that some people do not eat certain types of meat, or only eat meat that has been prepared in a certain way because of their religious beliefs. Buddhist: no meat or fish; Hindu: no beef; Jewish: Kosher meat, no pork or shellfish; Muslim: Halal meat, no pork; Sikh: no pork or beef. Share experiences of this as a class.